MW01193910

Hey Kids! Let's Visit Boston

Fun, Facts, and Amazing
Discoveries for Kids

Teresa Mills

Life Experiences Publishing

Contents

Welcome

Boston is a major United States city filled with parks, historical landmarks, museums, restaurants, shopping centers, universities, and many fun things to do. You will find tours, sports, history, and so much more! I love talking about history, so we will stroll through Boston from a historical perspective, learning about some of the famous places that shaped the United States and some of the more modern museums and tours!

This book is written as a fun fact guide about some attractions and sites in Boston. It includes some history interspersed with fun facts about things to do. The book can easily be enjoyed by younger children through reading it with them. You can visit Boston right from your own home! Whether you are preparing for a vacation with the family and want to learn more about the city or just want to learn a little more about Boston, this book is for you.

As you continue to learn more about Boston, I have some fun activity and coloring pages that you can download and print:

https://kid-friendly-family-vacations.com/bostonfun

When you have completed this book, I invite you to enjoy the other books in the series. We visit Washington DC, a Cruise Ship, New York City, London England, San Francisco, Savannah Georgia, Paris France, Charleston South Carolina, Chicago, Rome Italy, Philadelphia, San Diego, Seattle, Seoul South Korea, Atlanta, and Dublin Ireland!

Enjoy!

Teresa Mills

A Little About Boston

Boston was founded in 1630. The English Puritans were fleeing England and religious persecution. A fleet of 11 ships sailed towards Massachusetts from England on March 29, 1630, led by John Winthrop. The group originally settled in Charlestown along with another group that had arrived the previous year, but short fresh water supplies forced them to move across the river. The new settlement was named Boston after Boston in England (a market town in Lincolnshire).

Boston grew and developed quickly. Ship building was one of the first industries started in Boston with the first ship built in America sailing from Boston in 1631. Boston was also an important place for the whaling and fishing industries.

Boston grew on the educational front as well with the first public school opening in 1635 (Boston Latin School) and a college founded in 1636. The college was named Harvard in 1639. Another first for Boston was the first coffeehouse which opened in 1676. See the list below for more firsts in Boston.

Despite the smallpox outbreaks of 1702 and 1721, Boston continued to grow and prosper. Boston industries were also thriving although the first poorhouse (a place that is maintained at public expense to house needy persons) was opened in Boston in 1735.

Several buildings of note were built in Boston in the mid-1700s: The Old State House in 1713, the Old North Church in 1723, the Old South Meeting House in 1729, and Faneuil Hall in 1742.

Historically, Boston is famous for many events surrounding the American Revolution. In the mid-18th century, tensions were growing between the colonists and England, and British soldiers were stationed in Boston in 1768. At this time, events that shaped the American Revolution were happening around Boston: the Boston Massacre in 1770, the Boston Tea Party in 1773, the Midnight Ride of Paul Revere before the battles of Lexington and Concord in 1775 , the Boston Siege (after the battles of Lexington and Concord), and the Battle of Bunker Hill (Breed's Hill) in 1775.

U.S. Firsts in Boston

- First windmill – 1632 – Copp's Hill

- First U.S. public park – 1634 – Boston Common

- First public school – 1635 – Boston Latin

- First U.S. college – 1636 – Harvard

- First U.S. post office – 1639 – Boston Tavern was first post office in the country

- First U.S. public elementary school – 1639 – The Mather School

- First U.S. mail route – 1672 – between Boston and NYC

- First American restaurant – 1714 – Ye Olde Union Oyster House

- First U.S. lighthouse – 1721 – Boston Light

- First U.S. chocolate factory – 1765 – Baker Chocolate Factory

- First state constitution – 1780 – The Constitution of the Commonwealth of Massachusetts

- Oldest commissioned Navy warship launches – 1797 – the USS Constitution

- First African American meeting house – 1806 – The African Meeting House on Beacon Hill

- First U.S. swimming pool – 1827 – established

in Boston on July 23, 1827, by German American intellectuals Francis Lieber and Charles Follen

- First public school for African American children – 1835 – Abiel Smith School

- First college for women – 1837 – Mount Holyoke Female Seminary

- First city police department – 1837 – The Boston Police Department (BPD)

- First public library – 1854 – The Boston Public Library

- First telephone – 1876 – Alexander Graham Bell and Thomas A. Watson first transmitted sound over wires

- First Fig Newton – 1891 – Kennedy Biscuit Works in Cambridge, Massachusetts

- First U.S. subway system – 1897 – The Tremont Street Subway

- First World Series game – 1903 – Boston Americans of the American League against the Pittsburgh Pirates of the National League

And today? Boston is a very populous city bustling and growing but also respectful of its vast history.

So, are you ready? – Let's Visit Boston!

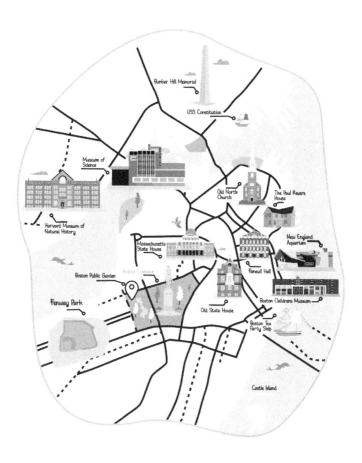

Map of Boston Attractions

Chapter 1

The Freedom Trail

The Freedom Trail is a 2.5-mile (4.0-kilometer) marked path throughout Boston. It highlights 16 spots around Boston that played a part in the history of the United States of America. The trail starts at the Boston Common and is marked with simple ground markers. The trail winds from the Boston Common through the North End to Bunker Hill. The nice thing about a walking tour like this is that you can spend as much time as you like at each stop along the trail.

The stops along the Freedom Trail include the following. Some of the stops are covered a little more in depth in other chapters if this book, but here is a quick description of what you will see on the trail.

Freedom Trail Marker

Boston Common

This is a public park, actually the oldest public park in the United States, dating back to 1634. Boston Common is 50 acres in size and was originally used by families of the colony as a cow pasture. Before the American Revolution, Boston Common was a camp for the British.

Massachusetts State House

This is the "new" State House in Boston. It was opened in 1798 and is currently in use as the seat of Massachusetts' government. This is essentially the capitol building of Massachusetts, housing the executive and legislative branches of the government.

Park Street Church

Park Street Church was the location of the original granary (a storehouse for animal feed or threshed grain) which was built in 1729. In addition to storing grain, the granary was also the place where the sails for the USS Constitution were created. The church was founded in this location in 1804 and is still an active evangelical congregation today.

Granary Burying Ground

The Granary Burying Ground is named for the granary (which is now the Park Street Church) that it is adjacent to. This burying ground is the third oldest in Boston, founded in 1660. These burying grounds are historically significant as they are the final resting place of three signers of the Declaration of Independence (Samuel Adams, John Hancock, and Robert Treat Paine), Paul Revere, and the five Boston Massacre victims as well as many others.

King's Chapel and King's Chapel Burying Ground

King's Chapel is one of Boston's oldest churches, dating back to 1686. The burying ground that is adjacent to the Chapel is not affiliated with the church but bears the same name. It was established in 1630 and is the oldest cemetery in Boston. Among those buried in the King's Chapel Burying Grounds is Mary Chilton (the first European woman to come to New England).

Boston Latin School / Benjamin Franklin Statue

The Boston Latin School was founded in 1635. It was the first public school founded in the United States. The statue of Benjamin Franklin marks the location of the original schoolhouse. Among notable Boston Latin alumni are five Declaration of Independence signers (Benjamin Franklin, Samuel Adams, Robert Treat Paine, John Hancock, and William Hooper), four Harvard presidents, and four Massachusetts governors.

Old Corner Bookstore

Boston's oldest commercial building was constructed in 1718. It was once home to Ticknor and Fields, a 19th century publishing giant. This company published some of the most well-known American literature including Louisa May Alcott's *Little Women*, Nathaniel Hawthorn's *The Scarlett Letter*, and the Atlantic Monthly.

Old South Meeting House

Famous as the organizing point for the Boston Tea Party in 1773, the Old South Meeting House is a church that was built in 1729. The meeting house was used for many public protest meetings against British actions from 1768-75.

Old State House

The Old State House, built in 1713, is the oldest surviving public building remaining in Boston. The Old State House is now a Freedom Trail museum. It houses many Revolution era objects and artifacts including tea salvaged from the Boston Tea Party, John Hancock's red velvet coat, and ammunition.

Boston Massacre Site

Boston was "occupied" by the British from 1768-1776 by over 2,000 soldiers. This caused tensions between the people of Boston and the British soldiers. The massacre was the result of a confrontation which left five Boston residents dead – shot by the British soldiers on March 5, 1770. The massacre was one of the first "fights" between the British and the colonists.

Faneuil Hall

Faneuil Hall was built in 1742 by Peter Faneuil as a central marketplace. Official town meetings were held there regularly. There were also meetings of concerned colonists that met in the assembly room there. These colonists would have ideas about freedom that laid the initial groundwork for the American Revolution.

Paul Revere House

The original three-story home was built in 1680. Paul Revere lived in this house at the time of his famous Midnight Ride in April of 1775.

Old North Church

If you are familiar with the Midnight Ride of Paul Revere, you will remember "One if by land, and two if by sea." There were 2 lanterns hung in the church's steeple signaling how the British were approaching Lexington and Concord.

Copp's Hill Burying Ground

One of the largest and oldest colonial cemeteries, Copp's Hill dates back to 1659. It was used by the British Army during the Revolutionary War Battle of Bunker Hill. Buried in the Copp's Hill Burying Grounds are preachers Cotton and Increase Mather, the Old North Church sexton Robert Newman (who helped hang lanterns in the church steeple on the night of Paul Revere's ride), builder of the USS Constitution Edmund Hartt and more.

USS Constitution

The USS Constitution is the oldest commissioned warship still on water. The ship is nicknamed "Old Ironsides" and earned the nickname during the war of 1812.

Bunker Hill Monument

A granite obelisk (a four-sided monument that has a pyramid shape at the top – just like the Washington Monument in Washington DC) was built to memorialize the Revolutionary efforts at Bunker Hill. Inside the monument, you can see great views of Boston.

Freedom Trail Map

Chapter 2

Boston Common

Boston Common is considered to be the oldest public park in the United States of America, established in 1634. The Common is 50 acres bound by five streets (Boylston Street, Charles Street, Beacon Street, Park Street, and Tremont Street). It was designated as a Boston Landmark in 1977 and a National Historic Landmark in 1987. The Freedom Trail's first stop is the Common.

The Boston Common has had many different functions over the years. In the early years (1630s) it was used as a cow pasture. The Common was used by the British as a camp prior to the Revolutionary War and then for public hangings up until 1817. It has been used for public demonstrations and riots like the one in 1713 where two hundred citizens reacted to a food shortage in the city. Around 1830, the Common started being used more like a park, and by 1836 the park was enclosed with an ornamental iron fence.

Boston Common

Today the Common is a lush green park with ballfields, tennis courts, swan boat rides, a frog pond (which is used for ice skating in the winter), and many monuments and memorials to mark the rich history of Boston.

Some of the Structures and Memorials in the Common

- The Brewer Fountain – an 1868 bronze sculpture located near Tremont Street. The sculpture represents mythological figures associated with water (Galatea, Acis, Amphitrite, and Neptune).

- The Soldiers and Sailor Monument – a Civil War memorial.

- Boston Massacre Monument – Dedicated in 1888, the memorial depicts the events before the massacre at the Old State House on March 5, 1770.

- The Parkman Bandstand – It is dedicated to George Francis Parkman who donated $5 million for the care of the Common and city parks.

Fun Facts About the Boston Common

- Bostonians gathered on the Common in 2006 to break the world record of the most Jack-o'-lanterns lit at the same time. The succeeded by lighting 30,126 Jack-o'-lanterns!

- There is a burying ground within the Common. The Central Burying Ground is in the Boylston Street section of the park. Famous people buried there include Samuel Sprague (Revolutionary War veteran and Boston Tea Party participant), his son Charles (poet), artist Gilbert Stuart, and composer William Billings.

- The original Tremont Subway Subway's (opened in 1897) Boylston Station and Park Street Station are both right below the Boston Common.

Chapter 3

Massachusetts State House

The Massachusetts State House (the new State House) is the state capitol of Massachusetts. It houses the legislative branches of the state government as well as the offices of the governor. The State House is located in the Beacon Hill section of Boston and sits across Beacon Street from the Boston Common. The land that the State House is on used to belong to John Hancock (Massachusetts' first elected governor). The State House is a stop on Boston's Freedom Trail.

The current (new) State House was built in 1798. Prior to this, the Massachusetts government was housed in the Old State House. The architect of the Massachusetts State House was Charles Bulfinch. He used designs form two buildings in London as his design model for the State House. One was William Chamber's

Somerset House and the other James Wyatt's Pantheon. In 1895, a major expansion took place with architect Charles Brigham. In 1917, the west and east wings were completed with architect firm Sturgis, Bryant, Chapman, and Andrews.

The Massachusetts State House

The dome of the State House is pretty distinctive. It was originally made of wood but that leaked. In 1802, Paul Revere's Copper Company covered the dome with copper sheathing. Later, in 1874 the dome was painted gray first, then light yellow. It was finally gilded with gold leaf. Between that time and 1997, the dome was painted gray again (during World War II). Then in 1997, the dome was once again gilded in 23K gold leaf. The cost of the gilding in 1997 was more than $300,000.

The interior of the State House is also a museum that reflects on the history of Massachusetts back to the colonial times. The State House is full of paintings, sculptures, and artifacts that commemorate people and events that helped shape Massachusetts and the United States of America.

Fun Facts About the State House

- The State House was used as a staged courthouse and hospital in the 1982 film *The Verdict*.

- The land that the State House was built on was a cow pasture owned by John Hancock.

- When the current governor of the state leaves office, the governor takes the "Long Walk" down the front staircase, across Beacon Street, and enters the Boston Common as a symbol of returning to Massachusetts as a private citizen.

Chapter 4

The Old State House

The Old State House is one of the oldest public buildings in the United States of America. As a historic building built in 1713 (then known as the Town House), it served as the home of the Massachusetts government until 1798. It is also a National Historic Landmark (designated in1960) and a Boston Landmark (designated in 1994). The Old State House is a stop on Boston's Freedom Trail.

The Old State House

In 1761, James Otis gave a speech in the Old State House that influenced public opinions that helped contribute to the American Revolution. After hearing the speech James Adams wrote, "Then and there ... the child of independence was born."

The Boston Massacre took place in the square to the east of the Old State House on March 5, 1770. The massacre was some of the first bloodshed in the years leading up to the American Revolution. Inside the museum is a Boston Massacre exhibit that chronicles this event. Artifacts from the event and an engraving by Paul Revere are part of this exhibit. Outside the state house is a circle of pavers that commemorates the location of the massacre.

Many historic announcements have taken place on the balcony of the Old State House. The first time the Declaration of Independence was read in Boston was from the balcony on July 18, 1776. The election of John Hancock as the first governor was also announced from this balcony in 1789.

Exhibits to see in the museum:

- The Old State House: A Hands-on History – an interactive exhibit exploring the changes in the building over the years.

- The Boston Massacre Exhibit – a multimedia exhibit chronicling the event.

- From Colony to Commonwealth – Explore the transition of Boston through the years.

- The Revolutionary Characters – Follow the lives of Bostonians in the 1770s.

- The Preservation of the Old State House – preservation efforts over the past years.

Fun Facts About the Old State House

- In 1789, President George Washington watched a parade in his honor from the Old State House.

- In 1960, the Boston Historical Sites Commission declared that the Old State House was the most important building built prior to the Declaration of Independence in America.

- After being built in 1713, it served as a merchant center and the seat of Boston colonial government.

Chapter 5

Faneuil Hall

Faneuil Hall is a meeting hall and marketplace. It was built in 1742 with funds provided by wealthy merchant Peter Faneuil who was in favor of a city-wide marketplace. Faneuil Hall and Marketplace is actually 4 markets in one – North and South Market, Quincy Market, and Faneuil Hall. It is one of the stops on Boston's Freedom Trail.

The meeting hall in Faneuil Hall was added as almost an afterthought, but it became almost invaluable to Boston. Among some of the famous discussions that happened in the meeting hall were the speeches against "taxation without representation" meetings to protest the Sugar Act of 1764 (a tax placed on sugar and molasses imported to all of the colonies which affected Boston and New England's exports of rum) and meetings to protest the Stamp Act of 1765 (a tax on all official documents in the colonies but not in England).

Faneuil Hall

Faneuil Hall is sometimes referred to as the "Cradle of Liberty" because of all of the pre-revolutionary discussions and decisions made there. In the small assembly room (meeting hall), many of the plans were made and organized for the Sons of Liberty's resistance to British rule. The Sons of Liberty was led by Samuel Adams.

Today, Faneuil Hall is a premier shopping and dining destination. The place is full of the hustle and bustle of activity including street performers, musicians, jugglers, acrobats, illusionists, comedians, and sword swallowers.

Fun Facts About Faneuil Hall

- There is a golden grasshopper weathervane on the top of Faneuil Hall. It has been in place there since 1742.

- The oldest restaurant in Faneuil Hall has been there since 1826. The restaurant is Durgin Park.

- Faneuil Hall hosts street performers in the marketplace. The performances started in the early 1970s. Faneuil Hall is one of the premier street performing venues in the world.

Chapter 6

Old North Church

The Old North Church is home to an active Episcopal Church congregation in Boston. The church was built in 1723 and is a National Historic Landmark. The Old North Church is the oldest surviving church building in Boston and is a part of Boston's Freedom Trail.

The Old North Church is most famous for the pre-Revolution events of April 18, 1775. The church sexton Robert Newman along with Captain John Pulling Jr. took two lanterns up to the steeple as instructed by Paul Revere. Paul told them that once he found out how the British were approaching Concord and Lexington – either by land or by sea – to display the lanterns in the steeple: "one if by land, two if by sea." The plan was prearranged before Paul's ride to warn the patriots in Lexington.

Old North Church Steeple with Paul Revere statue

On a more eerie note, archaeologists have estimated that there are close to 1,100 bodies buried in the basement of the church. The crypt was used from 1732 to 1860. Most of the burials were soldiers killed in the Battle of Bunker Hill. There is a behind the scenes tour of the church that explores the crypt.

The modern-day church offers educational programs that are free to educators. One that I find very interesting is "Chocolate and the Old North." It is a six-part lesson on the history of chocolate in Boston. Other programs are "History Mystery" (a three-part lesson about who held the lantern signals in the Old North Church), "Behind the Scenes Tour" (a half-hour video of the church's most interesting spaces), and "Cacao and

Colonial Chocolate" (a similar program to Chocolate and the Old North for high school students).

Fun Facts About the Old North Church

- The lanterns used the night of Paul Revere's ride are well preserved in the church today.

- The signal that started the American Revolution was sent from the steeple here.

- The original name of the church is Christ Church in the City of Boston. Old North is a nickname that is normally given to the oldest church in the North End. This church still holds that title!

Chapter 7

Paul Revere House

Built in 1680, the Paul Revere House is a colonial home in Boston's North End. This house was the home of American patriot Paul Revere at the time of the American Revolution. The Paul Revere House is a National Historic Landmark and a stop on Boston's Freedom Trail.

The Paul Revere House holds the honor of being the oldest house in Boston. It is a 3-story home very close to the waterfront where Paul's workshop was located. The Revere family lived in the home from 1770-1800. After he sold the home, it became a tenement (separate rooms to rent in one building). The downstairs was used for shops and businesses over the next years. Revere's great-grandson purchased the purchased the home in 1902 and restored it. It was opened to the public for tours in 1908.

Paul Revere House

Paul Revere is best known for his midnight ride in April 1775 to alert the colonial militia about the approach of the British forces towards Lexington and Concord. He was also a silversmith, an engraver, an industrialist (a person involved in the management of an industry), a member of the Sons of Liberty (a loosely organized group of colonists who were for the rights of the colonists), and an American founding father.

Paul was born in Boston's North End on December 21, 1734. He was the third of 12 children born to his parents. At the age of 13, he became a silversmith apprentice to his father. He had a different religious interest than his father. Revere's father attended Puritan services, but Paul eventually started attending West Church with the political John Mayhew. The difference of opinions in religion caused Paul and his father to have a fight after a disagreement once. So, Paul relented and returned to his father's church.

Paul eventually took over his family's silversmith business after his father's death, and he married Sarah Orne on August 4, 1757. Sarah Revere died in 1773, and Paul then married Rachel Walker. Sarah and Paul had 8 children and then Rachel and Paul had another 8 children. Of the children, 2 of Sarah's died young and 3 of Rachel's died young.

During all of this time, Paul Revere continued to be involved in the Sons of Liberty and keep his eyes on what was going on with the British. His Midnight Ride to warn the colonial militia of the British moving towards Lexington and Concord was one of the defining moments that marked the beginning of the Revolution.

Fun Facts About Paul Revere

- Paul never shouted, "The British are coming!" as he passed from town to town on his midnight ride. All of the colonists were actually British so that would not have made sense. What would make more sense would be to shout, "The Regulars are coming!" The Regulars was a term commonly used to refer to the British Army regiments.

- Paul Revere also worked as a dentist from time to time. He learned from John Baker, a dental surgeon who moved to Boston.

- Paul Revere was one of the leading participants of the Boston Tea Party. After the event, he rode to New York and Philadelphia to deliver the news of the "tea party."

Chapter 8

USS Constitution

The USS Constitution is a wooden-hulled frigate with three masts. It is a part of the United States Navy and the oldest ship that is still on water. She is also known as Old Ironsides – a nickname she earned during the War of 1812 against the British warship HMS Guerriere because it seemed like no cannon ball could damage the hull. The USS Constitution launched in 1797 as one of six frigates that were authorized by the Naval Act 0f 1794. The Naval Act authorized the building of the six frigates that would eventually become the US Navy of today. The Constitution is a part of Boston's Freedom Trail.

The Constitution was designed by Joshua Humphrey to handle very heavy guns. The ship was built for strength as the small US Navy did not have the size of European navies at the time. She was built in Boston's North End at Edmund Hartt's shipyard. The primary materials used in the construction were pine and oak. The hull of the USS Constitution was 21 inches (53.3 centimeters) thick.

The USS Constitution

The Constitution was constructed as a 44-gun frigate; however, she usually carried up to 50 guns. Unlike current Navy ships that have permanent guns, the guns and cannons on the frigates were portable and could be moved from place to place or from ship to ship. All of the guns now abord the Constitution are replicas and were placed on the ship during the 1927-1931 restoration.

Today, the Constitution often is seen in Boston Harbor for special anniversaries and commemorations. Across from the location of the USS Constitution is the USS Constitution Museum. The museum has some pretty cool hands-on experiences for visitors.

Fun Facts About the USS Constitution

- President George Washington chose the name USS Constitution for this ship from a list that included names such as President, Congress, Liberty, and Defender.

- The USS Constitution sailed in two bicentennial journeys under her own power – in 1997 to celebrate her 200th birthday and again in 2012 to celebrate the anniversary of her victory against Guerriere.

- Oliver Wendell Holmes's poem "Old Ironsides" built up public sentiment for the ship when she was condemned as unseaworthy in 1830. Because of that public sentiment, the ship was preserved for rebuilding.

Chapter 9

Bunker Hill Memorial

The Bunker Hill Battle Monument stands 221 feet (67.4 meters) tall atop Breed's Hill in Boston. It is an obelisk (a four-sided tapering monument ending in a pyramid shape at the top – like the Washington Monument in Washington DC) constructed from granite. The monument took over 17 years (1825-1842) to build. The Bunker Hill Monument is a part of Boston's Freedom Trail.

Taking place on June 17, 1775, the Battle of Bunker Hill was the first major American Revolution battle. A large portion of the battle actually took place on the larger Breed's Hill, and that is where the monument is located today. Breed's Hill is located on the southern portion of the Charlestown Peninsula.

The American colonists had heard that the British planned to fortify the peninsula, so they decided to get there first. By getting there first, the Americans could fortify the peninsula and provide a threat to hopefully get the British to leave Boston. The Americans constructed a redoubt (a temporary fortification sometimes built around existing forts to protect soldiers that were outside the main fort) on Breed's Hill. The British were amazed when they saw the fortifications, so they set out to reclaim the peninsula.

There were about 1,500 Americans under the leadership of General Putnam and Colonel Prescott when the nearly 2,400 British soldiers under General Howe attacked. The colonists held off two attacks, but after the third attack thy retreated. The battle killed or wounded 450 colonists and over 1,000 British soldiers.

Bunker Hill Monument

Fun Facts About the Battle at Bunker Hill

- To help preserve the colonists' ammunition, Colonel Prescott told his militia, "Don't fire until you see the whites of their eyes."

- The battle was one of the bloodiest of the Revolution.

- 10 miles south of Bunker Hill, there was a 7-year-old future US president watching the battle. John Quincy Adams stood with his mother watching the smoke rise from the battle.

Chapter 10

Castle Island and Fort Independence

Fort Independence located on Castle Island is a pentagonal five-bastioned fort (a polygon design with bastions – a structure extending outward from the wall – at the corners of the fort). Bastion forts are also sometimes called star forts. The fort is made of granite and is one of the oldest fortified installations in the US. It provides harbor defense for Boston.

Castle Island is a peninsula on the southern part of Boston. There have been fortifications there since 1634. Today, it is a 22-acre recreation site as well as the location of Fort Independence.

The first fortification on Castle Island was simply called "The Castle." It was rebuilt several times and finally replaced in 1692 with what was called Castle William. During the American Revolution at the time of the

Siege of Boston, Castle William was a base of military operations for the British. After the British left Boston in March of 1776, the Castle was destroyed.

The fort was rebuilt by American forces after it was destroyed and named Fort Adams. In December of 1797 the fort was renamed Fort Independence. The current fort (which was actually the 8th build of a fort at this location) was built between 1833 and 1851 and is on the National Register of Historic Places.

Fort Independence

Fun Facts About Castle Island and Fort Independence

Today, Fort Independence is a Massachusetts State Park.

From Castle Island, you have great views of the Boston Harbor and Logan Airport – great for watching planes land and take off.

Castle Island has many great playgrounds and beaches to enjoy.

Chapter 11

Boston Tea Party Ship & Museum

The Boston Tea Party was, for all intents and purposes, a political protest. The American colonists in Boston were angry and frustrated at the British for imposing a tax on them without there being any colonist members of the British Parliament ("taxation without representation"). So, in protest, the colonists dumped 342 chests of tea that was imported to Boston by the British East India Company into the Boston Harbor! This occurred on December 16, 1773. The "tea party" turned out to be a rallying cry across the 13 colonies to fight for their independence.

There was quite a bit that led up to the Boston Tea Party. The British government was deep in debt, so they imposed a series of taxes on the American colonists. The Stamp Act of 1765 taxed all printed paper used. The

Townshend Acts of 1767 then went further and taxed paper, glass, paint, and tea. All of this taxation created tensions between the colonists in Boston and the British that were there. One of the first brawls ended with the Boston Massacre where five colonists were killed and six were wounded. Eventually, the British repealed all of the taxes except the tax on tea. In protest, the colonists then boycotted (stopped doing business with) the British East India Company and smuggled in Dutch tea, leaving the British East India Company facing bankruptcy (a legal process for companies who can no longer pay their debts).

So, in May of 1773, the British Parliament passed the Tea Act. This allowed the British East India Company to sell their tea duty free (without taxes) and much cheaper, but the tea was still taxed when it reached the colonies. As you can imagine, tea smuggling became even more common even though it was more expensive now. Two prominent smugglers were John Hancock and Samuel Adams, and they were definitely against the "taxation without representation."

Adams, Hancock, and other patriots – Patrick Henry, Benedict Arnold, and Paul Revere – were also against the taxes. They met with other Sons of Liberty members on the morning of December 16, 1773, and they voted to refuse to allow the tea from three ships that had just arrived full of British East India Company tea to be unloaded, sold, stored, or used. They also voted to refuse to pay the taxes. Governor Thomas Hutchinson (a royal governor of the British province of Massachusetts in Boston) refused to send the ships back to Britain and ordered that the tax be paid and the ship unloaded. The colonists refused, and a there was not a compromise. Later that night, a large group of men boarded the ships and threw the 342 chests of tea overboard into the Boston Harbor.

King George III and the British Parliament imposed some pretty strict rules on the colonists after the tea party called the "Coercive Acts." This led to the colonists forming the First Continental Congress between September 5 and October 26, 1774. The congress discussed many things, but mainly it was convened to react to the Coercive Acts (known in America as the Intolerable Acts). Tensions continued to rise as both the British and the American Colonists tried to negotiate further, eventually leading to the "shot heard round the World" in the battles of Concord and Lexington.

The Boston Tea Party Ship & Museum has multi-sensory exhibits that help visitors understand the tensions that the colonists felt. You can see re-enactments of the events leading up to the "tea party" and the party itself, discovering the true story behind these historical events. At the museum is a replica of the British East India Company tea ships!

Boston Tea Party Ship & Museum

Fun Facts About the Boston Tea Party

- George Washington was not thrilled personally about the Boston Tea Party. He wrote of his disapproval in "their conduct in destroying the Tea." Publicly, he supported the cause.

- Benjamin Franklin thought that the cost of the tea should be reimbursed to the British.

- The meeting held before the tea party was held at the Old South Meeting House.

Chapter 12

Boston Public Garden

The Boston Public Garden is adjacent to the Boston Common, but it was established in 1837, more than 200 years after the Common. The park was the first botanical garden (a park where plants are grown for displaying to the public or for studying) in the United States. The Public Garden is much more decorative than the Boston Common and offers a retreat from the busy city.

The land west of the Common was purchased by the city in 1824 and set apart for future public use. In 1837, Horace Gray and a group of horticulturists got permission to create a public botanical garden on the land. The garden remained the Botanic Public Garden in Boston for quite a while. Then in 1859, the city started looking at various ways to use the property as a park. A design competition was held, with George Meacham's design of a curved path system formal garden with a pond and flowerbeds winning. By 1880, the park was fenced with a cast-iron fence. There was a suspension bridge that spanned the pond, and trees and plants were numerous. The first sculptures were placed in the park in 1867, and the swan boats began "swimming" in 1877.

The Boston Common and the Boston Public Garden form the northern end of a chain of parks called the Emerald Necklace. The Emerald Necklace was designed by Frederick Law Olmsted and stretches across 1,100 acres in Boston and Brookline, connecting parks by parkways and waterways.

In addition to the pond that houses the swan boats and all of the trees and flowers throughout the garden, there are many statues and sculptures along the pathways. Some of the statues that you will find in the garden are:

- A statue of George Washington on horseback – a bronze statue 16 feet (4.9 meters) tall on a granite pedestal that is also 16 feet (4.9 meters) tall.

- The Ether Monument – memorializing the first use of ether as an anesthetic. The granite and red marble monument stands 30 feet (9 meters) tall. The figures in the carving tell the parable of the Good Samaritan.

- Make Way for Ducklings – a set of bronze statues from the book of the same name.

- A footbridge crossing the lagoon.

- A Japanese garden lantern – dating back to 1587, the lantern is one of the oldest of its kind still around.

Make Way for Ducklings

Fun Facts About the Boston Public Garden

- The "Make Way for Ducklings" statue is the most famous in the gardens and may be one of the most famous in the entire city.

- A pair of real swans call the pond home during the warm months. In May, there is a parade to welcome the swans back home to the pond.

- Every May since 1840, tulips bloom in the garden (except when weather prevents the plantings). The beautiful blooms are around for almost a month and are a favorite spot for photographers.

Chapter 13

Fenway Park

Fenway Park is the ballpark of the Boston Red Sox baseball team. The park, built in 1912 with major expansions and renovations in 1934, 2002-2011, 2017, and 2022 is Major League Baseball's oldest stadium. The stadium is in the Fenway-Kenmore neighborhood of Boston and doesn't have a whole lot of room for expansion. The stadium opened with a seating capacity of close to 35,000 and has just under a seating capacity of 40,000 today, making it one of the smaller MLB stadiums.

Fenway Park was named by John I Taylor who purchased the land for the park in 1911 and developed the baseball field. The stadium's Fenway-Kenmore neighborhood takes its name from the Back Bay Fens also known as "The Fens." The Fens is an urban marshland or fen (a peat-accumulating marshland) park that is also a part of Boston's Emerald Necklace of parks, just like the Boston

Public Garden and the Boston Common. Given all of this history, the name Fenway Park makes sense.

Aerial view of Fenway Park

Some of the most interesting characteristics of this park include:

The Green Monster

The dimensions of Fenway Park and the way that it fits into the already existing street structure create a unique shape to the field. The Green Monster is a 37 foot (11.3 meters) tall wall in the left field. The wall is painted green and has been since 1947. Before 1947, the wall was covered with advertisements. The wall is between 310 and 315 feet (94.5-96 meters) from home plate. The average left field line for MLB fields is 403.5 feet (123 meters)., so the left field is shorter than most. The height of the wall prevents a lot of line drive homeruns that hit the wall.

Monster Seats

Before the 2003 baseball season, the Green Monster had nets draped atop the wall to catch balls hit that direction. In 2002, seats were added to the top of the wall. These seats are affectionately called the monster seats!

The Manual Scoreboard

A manually operated scoreboard was installed at Fenway in 1934, and it is still used today. The scoreboard is located at the bottom of the Green Monster. There are three operators inside the wall who keep the scoreboard updated during games.

The Fisk Pole

The name given to the foul pole that sits on the Green Monster, the left field wall. On October 22, 1975, Carlton Fisk (a Red Sox catcher) hit a fastball from Pat Darcy of the Cincinnati Reds and it hit the foul pole. The hit was the last of a 12-inning game – game six of the 1975 World Series – winning the game for Boston and sending the series into a 7th game.

The Pesky Pole

This is the right field foul pole in Fenway. It is only 302 feet (92 meters) from home plate, the shortest outfield distance for any MLB field. The pole is named after Johnny Pesky who hit some of his six homeruns close to this foul pole.

The Lone Red Seat

At Section 42, Row 37, Seat 21 – 502 feet from home plate – you will find the lone red seat. A ball was hit by Ted Williams in 1946 that went directly to that seat and hit the gentleman sitting there in the head (Joe Boucher from Albany). This was the longest homerun ever hit in Fenway Park.

Fun Facts About Fenway Park

- In 1914, there was a parade of elephants held at Fenway Park. There were well over 50,000 kids at the park that day to see the parade.

- The first player to hit a homerun at Fenway that was not a Red Sox player was Babe Ruth.

- Fenway Park has a manually operated scoreboard still in operation today. It is located right below the "Green Monster."

Fenway Park

Chapter 14

Museum of Science

The Museum of Science (MoS) opened in 1830 as the Boston Society of Natural Science. Later, the museum was also called the Boston Museum of Natural History. The Museum of Science is an indoor zoo and a science museum located along the Charles River in Science Park. The museum was renamed the Museum of Science in 1939.

The founders of the museum were a group of men who wanted to share scientific interests. The Museum of Science has over 700 exhibits, and the zoo portion, which is accredited by the Association of Zoos and Aquariums, houses over 100 animals. You will also find a planetarium, an IMAX theater, 4D films, and live presentations throughout the day. In addition, while at the museum, you will see some pretty cool exhibits in the three level, multi-winged museum.

Some of the cool exhibits around the museum include:

Science Based Exhibits

- Engineering Design Workshop

- Exploring AI

- Theater of Electricity

- Seeing is Deceiving – optical illusions

- Math Moves!

- To the Moon

- Take a Closer Look

- Natural Mysteries

Animal and Biology Exhibits

- Garden Walk and Insect Zoo

- A Bird's World

- New England Habitats

- Hall of Human Life

- Bees

- Axolotls

Fun Facts About the Museum of Science

- The museum hosted the *Lord of the Rings Motion Picture Trilogy: The Exhibition* from August to October 2004.

- *Harry Potter: The Exhibition* was at the museum from October 2009 – February 2010.

- In 2016, Michael Bloomberg (the former mayor of New York City) gave the Museum of Science a gift of $50 million. He said about the museum and his gift, "I know how important this Museum is and what an impact it can have on young people — because I was one of those young people."

Chapter 15

New England Aquarium

The New England Aquarium overlooks the Boston Harbor and hosts more than 1.3 million visitors a year. The aquarium opened for business in 1969. The Giant Ocean Tank, which is a large circular ocean tank, opened in 1970. At that time, this was the largest tank of that type in the world.

Some of the cool things to do and see at the New England Aquarium are:

The Giant Ocean Tank

A four-story tall circular ocean tank that is set up as a Caribbean coral reef. The Giant Ocean Tank is home to over 1,000 sea animals including barracuda, loggerhead sea turtles, moray eels, and other coral reef fish.

Sea Turtle at New England Aquarium

Penguin Exhibit

The penguin exhibit surrounds the Giant Ocean Tank and is home to two species of penguins. The southern rockhopper penguins have yellow feathers on top of their heads and grown to about 18 inches (45.7 centimeters) in height, weighing between 5 and 10 pounds (2.2 to 4.5 kilograms). The African penguin makes a sound much like a donkey's bray and grow up to 25 inches (63.5 centimeters) tall, weighing between 5 and 9 pounds (2.2 to 4 kilograms).

Shark and Ray Touch Tank

The shark and ray touch tank is designed with a mangrove theme. The tank is home to cownose rays, Atlantic rays, and epaulette sharks. Cownose rays grow up to 48 inches (121.9 centimeters) wide. Atlantic stingrays are much smaller, growing up to 14 inches (35.6 centimeters) wide. The epaulette shark is a small species that usually remains under 3.3 feet (1 meter) in length

Simons Theater

The Simons Theater is a large screen theater that is open seven days a week. The films shown are normally nature based and last close to 40 minutes each. The screen in the Simons Theater is six stories tall.

Fun Facts About the New England Aquarium

- Over 80 penguins have been hatched and raised at the New England Aquarium.

- The Giant Ocean Tank is so big that it was built first, and the rest of the Aquarium was built around it.

- The shark and ray touch tank in the New England Aquarium is one of the largest of its kind on the East Coast.

Chapter 16

Boston Children's Museum

The Boston Children's Museum opened in 1913 and is dedicated to the education of children. The museum is located on Children's Wharf, which is a part of Boston's Harbor Walk. Boston Children's Museum is the second oldest in the United States, second only to the Brooklyn Children's Museum, which opened in 1899.

The museum emphasizes hands on interactions in the exhibits. Some cool things you will find there are:

Bubbles

Experiment with creating bubbles of every size with bubble making tools. Kids and adults can experiment side by side making bubbles.

Investigate

Explore the natural world with hands-on science activities like crawling under a turtle tank.

Kid Power

Work together with your family to learn how to move your bodies and choose healthy foods. Climb walls, shoot basketball hoops, or pedal to light up a sign.

New Balance Climb

A 3-story climbing sculpture right in the lobby. Kids and adults alike can climb and explore.

Raceways

Explore the laws of motion with a golf ball and different slides.

Arthur and Friends

Explore the world of Marc Brown's world of Arthur with different imagination boosting play areas.

Fantastic Forts

Use your imagination and build a fort to play in – then build another.

Fun Facts About the Boston Children's Museum

- The Hood Milk Bottle is a fixture in front of the Children's Museum. The bottle is 40 feet (12 meters) tall. If it could hold milk, it would hold 58,620 gallons (221,900 liters) of milk. It's an iconic attraction on the Children's Wharf, and ice cream is sold there.

- The museum has an exhibit called Boston Black where kids can explore Boston neighborhoods, visiting iconic places in each. Kids learn about diversity and different ethnic backgrounds.

- At the museum, you can take part in hour-long family workshops set up as STEAM (science, technology, engineering, art, and math) learning opportunities. Past events have been Kitchen Science and Critter Days.

Chapter 17

Boston Harborwalk

The Boston Harborwalk is basically a pathway along the edge of the water that connects most of the Boston Harbor. The pathway stretches for a continuous 43 miles. People visiting Boston can walk along the Harborwalk to visit restaurants, museums, and parks or to just stroll along the waterfront.

The Harborwalk also connects with some other trails that had already been built. The Freedom Trail, the Emerald Necklace, several greenways, and bike paths connect to the Harborwalk to make it really easy to get around Boston. The project has been in the works since 1984.

Boston Harborwalk

The walk extends from Dorchester (south of Boston) to the North End and Charlestown, passing through downtown Boston along the way. Points of interest along the Harborwalk include:

- Dorchester (Columbia Point)

- University of Massachusetts – Boston

- John F. Kennedy Presidential Library and Museum

- South Boston

- Boston Children's Museum

- Castle Island

- Downtown

- North End

- Copp's Hill

- Faneuil Hall and Quincy Market

- New England Aquarium

- Site of the Boston Tea Party

- North of Charles River

- Charlestown

- Bunker Hill Monument

- Paul Revere Park

Fun Facts About the Boston Harborwalk

- The Harborwalk connects 8 Boston neighborhoods: Dorchester, South Boston, Fort Point Channel, Seaport District, Wharf District, North End, Charlestown, East Boston.

- There are nine public beaches along the walk.

- The Friends of the Boston Harborwalk (FBHW) was established in 2014. This is a group of volunteers who give tours and sponsor clean-ups along the Harborwalk.

Chapter 18

Harvard Museum of Natural History

The Harvard Museum of Natural History is located on the Harvard University campus. It was created in 1998 and is the location to see displays from three of the University's research museums: Harvard Mineralogical Museum, Museum of Comparative Zoology, and Harvard University Herbaria.

The museum is a part of the Harvard Museums of Science and Culture. The other three museums are the Peabody Museum of Archaeology and Ethnology, Collection of Historical Scientific Instruments, and the Harvard Museum of the Ancient Near East. The Harvard Museum of Natural History is connected to the Peabody Museum of Archaeology and Ethnology, and both museums are included on the same admission ticket.

Harvard Museum of Natural History

One of the most fascinating exhibits in the Museum of Natural History is the "Ware Collection of Blaschka Glass Models of Plants" or more simply the "Glass Flowers." The "Glass Flowers" exhibit is a collection of flower models designed by father and son team Leopold and Rudolf Blaschka. The men created over 4,300 glass models of approximately 780 different plant varieties. The team also created glass models of terrestrial and marine animals. These glass sculptures are also on display at the museum.

Other cool exhibits include:

The Rockefeller Beetles

David Rockefeller's childhood imagination grew into a lifelong passion. For 90 years, David Rockefeller collected beetles from all over the world, amassing a collection of over 150,000 beetles. This display is in the arthropods section of the museum.

Great Mammal Hall

One of the most dramatic exhibits in the museum, the Great Mammal Hall is a two-story museum gallery. Here you will find a full-size giraffe, a narwhal, a bison, and whale skeletons.

Birds of the World

A display of more than 10,000 species of birds.

Arthropods: Creatures That Rule

The latest information on the study of arthropods
(insects, spiders - invertebrates that do not have an
internal skeleton or backbone) and their extraordinary
lives.

Chapter 19

Walking Tours

Boston is easy to get around, and as we have seen, there are many trails, gardens, and pathways already set up for walking. So, walking tours are one of the best ways to get more out of this great city!

Here are a few of the tour companies offering walking tours:

Free Tours by Foot

Free Tours by Foot offers tours of Boston at no cost up front. The tours run on a pay-what-you-like model. In Boston, the company offers a 2-hour walking tour along the Freedom Trail, themed tours such as *Rum, Riots, and Writers* (an alternative history tour of Boston revealing secret histories as well as some writers who helped shape history), and *Beacon Hill Crime* (learn more about the Boston Strangler). The company also offers ghost tours.

Boston Town Crier

The Boston Town Crier offers Freedom Trail tours with tour guides in period costume. The tours cover the first 11 stops along the Freedom Trail (from the Boston Common to Faneuil Hall), taking about 90 minutes. The tour guides portray historical characters from the history of Boston. At this time, your tour guides will either be James Otis (famous for the cry "Taxation without representation is tyranny"), John Gill (a printer of the colonial newspaper "The Boston Journal"), or Nabbie Cranch Smith (a fictional character who was a friend of Jon and Abigail Adams).

Ghosts and Gravestones Boston

The company offers a ghost walking tour of Boston. They explore some of Boston's most haunted sites and two of the three burying grounds in town. Be prepared for fun, scares, and ghost stories.

The Revolutionary Story Tour

This is a half day narrative walking tour of Boston. You will visit the most popular tourist sites and neighborhoods, following the events leading up to the Revolution in chronological order and with history. This tour does more than just scratch the surface of all the Boston offers historically!

Walking Boston

This company offers private tours with guide Ben Edwards, visiting the Freedom Trail sites on a fun and unique story-telling tour. Ben is also a children's author of *One April in Boston,* about the beginnings of the American Revolution. Ben's tours include an eBook and audio version of his book.

Chapter 20

Bike and Segway Tours

For the more adventurous at heart, what about a tour of Boston on a bike or a Segway? Biking is a great way to get out and move around; you will cover more ground than on a walking tour and get a little exercise. A Segway (a two-wheeled self-balancing personal transportation machine) tour can be even more adventurous! Both types of tours are available in Boston. Here is a little more information:

Bike Tours – Urban AdvenTours

Urban AdvenTours offers bike tours as well as bike rentals in Boston. Bike tours are offered daily, and e-bikes are available as an upgrade. Their list of tours includes four popular choices including a family friendly *Tour de Boston*, which is completely on bike paths along the Charles River, making the trip a little easier for kids.

Other options include a *City View Tour* (a 10- to 12-mile tour through six different Boston neighborhoods), a *Tour de Cambridge* (a 12- to 14-mile tour around Cambridge), and the *Emerald Necklace Tour* (a 15+ mile tour through Boston's green spaces).

Segway Tours – Boston Segway Tours

Boston Segway Tours offers a one-hour or a two-hour tour of Boston. The one-hour tours go into the center of Boston at the Boston Common area then make their way to the Harbor. The two-hour tour follows many of the Freedom Trail highlights, then through the Financial District to the Boston Harbor. The tour then ventures out into Cambridge, Beacon Hill, Back Bay, and finish along the Rose F. Kennedy Greenway back to the starting point. The tours cover history and current events in Boston to give you a complete overview!

Note: to ride a Segway, you must be 14 years old and weigh at least 100 pounds.

I hope you enjoyed your trip to Boston! I have a fun puzzle and coloring page download to go along with the book. This fun addition is free to download here:

https://kid-friendly-family-vacations.com/bostonfun

Please consider adding a review to help other readers learn more about Boston whether traveling or learning from home. Thanks!

kid-friendly-family-vacations.com/review-boston

Also By Teresa Mills and Kid Friendly Family Vacations

Hey Kids! Let's Visit Washington DC

Hey Kids! Let's Visit A Cruise Ship

Hey Kids! Let's Visit New York City

Hey Kids! Let's Visit London England

Hey Kids! Let's Visit San Francisco

Hey Kids! Let's Visit Savannah Georgia

Hey Kids! Let's Visit Paris France

Hey Kids! Let's Visit Charleston South Carolina

Hey Kids! Let's Visit Chicago

Hey Kids! Let's Visit Rome Italy

Hey Kids! Let's Visit Boston

Hey Kids! Let's Visit Philadelphia

Hey Kids! Let's Visit San Diego

Hey Kids! Let's Visit Seattle

Hey Kids! Let's Visit Seoul South Korea

Hey Kids! Let's Visit Atlanta

Hey Kids! Let's Visit Dublin Ireland

More from Kid Friendly Family Vacations

BOOKS

Books to help build your kids / grandkids life experiences through travel and learning
https://kid-friendly-family-vacations.com/books

COLORING AND ACTIVITY PAGKAGES

Coloring pages, activity books, printable travel journals, and more in our Etsy shop
https://kid-friendly-family-vacations.com/etsy

RESOURCES FOR TEACHERS

Resources for teachers on Teachers Pay Teachers
https://kid-friendly-family-vacations.com/tpt

It is our mission to help you build your children's and grand-children's life experiences through travel. Not just traveling with your kids... building their Life Experiences"! Join our community here:
https://kid-friendly-family-vacations.com/join

Acknowledgements

Proofreading / Editing

Katie Erickson – KatieEricksonEditing.com

Cover Photos

Freedom Trail Sign – © superbo / depositphotos.com

Massachusetts State House – © lunamarina / depositphotos.com

Old North Church Steeple – © YAYImages / depositphotos.com

USS Constitution – © marcorubino / depositphotos.com

Photos in Book

Freedom Trail Sign – © superbo / depositphotos.com

Boston Common Park – © rabbit75_dep / depositphotos.com

Massachusetts State House – © lunamarina / depositphotos.com

Old State House – © a_oldman / depositphotos.com

Faneuil Hall – © f11photo / depositphotos.com

Old North Church Steeple – © YAYImages / depositphotos.com

Paul Revere House – © zrfphoto / depositphotos.com

USS Constitution – © marcorubino / depositphotos.com

Bunker Hill Memorial – © Hackman / depositphotos.com

Fort Independence - © dbvirago / depositphotos.com

Boston Tea Party Museum – © edella / depositphotos.com

Boston Public Garden – Make Way for Ducklings – © dimamorgan12 / depositphotos.com

Fenway Park – Arial View – © 4kclips / depositphotos.com

Fenway Park – © Brittany Duckett – Brittany Bee Travel

New England Aquarium – sea turtle – © katkami / depositphotos.com

Boston Harborwalk – © appalachianview / depositphotos.com

Harvard Museum of Natural History – © PapaBravo / depositphotos.com

About the Author

Teresa Mills is the bestselling author of the "Hey Kids! Let's Visit..." Book Series for Kids! Teresa's goal through her books and website is to help parents / grandparents who want to build the life experiences of their children / grandchildren through travel and learning activities.

She is an active mother and Mimi. She and her family love traveling in the USA, and internationally too! They love exploring new places, eating cool foods, and having yet another adventure as a family! With the Mills, it's all about traveling as family.

In addition to traveling, Teresa enjoys reading, hiking, biking, and helping others.

Join in the fun at

kid-friendly-family-vacations.com

Made in the USA
Middletown, DE
15 May 2025

75577074R00060